Green Peas in Cream

Suzanne I. Barchers

Consultants

Robert C. Calfee, Ph.D.
Stanford University

P. David Pearson, Ph.D.
University of California, Berkeley

Publishing Credits

Dona Herweck Rice, *Editor-in-Chief*
Lee Aucoin, *Creative Director*
Sharon Coan, M.S.Ed., *Project Manager*
Jamey Acosta, *Editor*
Robin Erickson, *Designer*
Cathie Lowmiller, *Illustrator*
Robin Demougeot, *Associate Art Director*
Heather Marr, *Copy Editor*
Rachelle Cracchiolo, M.S.Ed., *Publisher*

Teacher Created Materials

5301 Oceanus Drive
Huntington Beach, CA 92649-1030
http://www.tcmpub.com

ISBN 978-1-4333-2916-6

© 2012 Teacher Created Materials, Inc.
Printed in Malaysia. THU001.48806

When Pete needs to eat, green food can't be beat.

He eats beans that are green. He eats green peas in cream.

He eats greens from a beet. (He will not eat green meat.)

He eats kiwi and seaweed, green apples, and dill weed.

He likes leeks with his meal. (He will not eat green veal.)

He likes most jelly beans as long as they're green.

He eats lime and its peel. (He will not eat green eel.)

He drinks cups of green tea.

Then Pete says, "Please. May I have more Sweets? This meal is a treat!"

Mint ice cream is neat. That is all he can eat.

As you have just seen, Pete likes food to be green.

He licks the plate clean to get all that is green.

Decodable Words

and	dill	ice	meal	Pete
as	drinks	in	meat	plate
be	eat	its	mint	please
beans	eats	just	more	seen
beat	eel	leeks	most	sweets
beet	get	licks	neat	tea
can	green	likes	needs	treat
clean	greens	lime	not	veal
cream	he	long	peas	weed
cups	his	may	peel	will

Sight Words

a	one
all	that
are	then
as	this
from	to
have	when
I	with
is	you

Challenge Words

apples	kiwi
can't	says
food	seaweed
jelly	they're

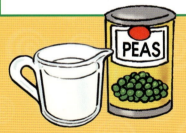

15

Extension Activities

Discussion Questions

- What are some of the green foods that Pete does not like? (meat, veal, and eel.)
- Which of the green foods do you like?
- Which of the green foods do you not like?
- What is your favorite color food? Why?

Exploring the Story

- Talk about the words *beat*, *meal*, and *meat*. Write them so you can see how they are spelled. Discuss how the letters *ea* can make the long vowel sound heard at the beginning of the word *eat*. Find other words in the story that have *ea* representing the sound of long vowel *e* (*beans*, *clean*, *cream*, *eat*, *neat*, *peas*, *please*, *seaweed*, *tea*, *treat*, and *veal*).

- Create green critters out of green fruits and vegetables. Use toothpicks to put the critters together. Consider foods such as cucumbers for the body, peas for the facial features, parsley for the hair, lime slices for the ears, and green beans for the arms and legs.

- This old clapping game was based on porridge made of peas. While facing each other and reciting the rhyme, two players repeat the following clapping pattern with each word: their own hands together on the word *Pease*, each other's right hand on the word *porridge*, hands together on the word hot, each other's left hand in the pause before the second line. Repeat this process faster and faster while reciting the rhyme.

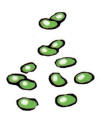

Pease porridge hot.
Pease porridge cold.
Pease porridge in the pot
Nine days old.
Some like it hot.
Some like it cold.
Some like it in the pot
Nine days old.